Ulrich
Seidl

In the
Basement

Ulrich Seidl In the Basement

Claus Philipp and
Astrid Wolfig (eds.)

Olaf Möller
Franz Schuh
Ute Woltron
Herbert Lachmayer
Claus Philipp
Markus Keuschnigg

Translated
by Robert Gray

Benteli

Contents

The Stop Key as Shutter Button

A Foreword
Claus Philipp

Like a sponge you soak up the Now / and then process it / when the Now has been gone long enough / to know what it is capable of…

Der Nino aus Wien, "It's Always about Completion"

What
can
the Now do? How can it be distilled into something—a work of art, perhaps—that is more than the Now? In the case of this book, from the film's original 120,000-plus individual images exactly 58 were chosen and assembled here. Of course, that may be somewhat hyperbolic, but a film like Ulrich Seidl's "In the Basement" (2014) draws its movement and momentum from the constant succession of 24 images per second.

Like
the
film "In the Basement", this book came into being at the editing table. Ulrich Seidl—the Austrian filmmaker, observer of his fellow humans, surveyor and author—used its stop key like the shutter release of a camera. He sought—and found—images or tableaux that, wrested from their filmic context, create their own stories, becoming autonomous outlines for worlds and times.

As such, this photo album is anything but just another "book about the film." It should, instead, exist for itself as an autonomous variation about a claustrophile society—an underground that, at least in Austria, cannot simply be equated with fringe groups or minorities.

Subversion:
In
its lexical sense the word means little more than "concealed or underground activity whose goal is the overthrow of an existing order." Considering the subterranean inhabitants of Seidl's tableaux, we might wonder if certain forms of going underground (and underground living spaces) don't represent the most recent and unconventional attempts by people to stabilize their undermined lives.

Provocation, on the other hand (a criticism often leveled at Ulrich Seidl and his works, which have been dogged by controversy from day one): Film director Christoph Schlingensief —a big Seidl fan—once said he had no idea what it meant to be a provocateur, that he was himself at most a "self-provocateur." When he found that something in his work proved, for some, difficult to accept or even unreasonable, often it was because that something had irritated and made him question himself as an artist and citizen and human being.

"I
am
the cause," wrote Thomas Bernhard. The statement may also apply to the self-provocateur Ulrich Seidl, regardless of whether he is framing his scenes down to the millimeter, letting the camera roll, or simply pressing the stop key in order to capture a single, autonomous image. Which is how 58 images were compiled for this book. The texts that accompany them are impulses toward and signs of observation or thought processes with an open ending. "It's Always about Completion" is the title of a song by the popular Austrian singer-songwriter Der Nino aus Wien. There may nonetheless be an "afterwards," something set in motion—even if only attempts at awareness, at self-awareness. Beauty too. Perhaps.

Your finger's the most dangerous part of your gun.

Handgun Parts
Bolt Action Rifle Parts
Cartridge Components
Firing Sequence
Sight Alignment / Adjustment
Cartridge Components
Firing Sequence

The Chorus of the Slaves

Olaf Möller

In the first days of June 2014, the word “Kellari” (cellar) screamed out from the front page of every tabloid in Finland. The bodies of five newborns had been discovered in a basement in Oulu. Five times a woman had gotten pregnant, five times she had managed to hide this from everyone around her—or at least, that’s what they claim—five times she had given birth in her home, five times... what happened next is obvious. According to DNA tests, the children were not all from different fathers. The name Marc Dutroux rises from the depths of our collective memory, and then too that of Josef Fritzl.

Many
people
assumed that Ulrich Seidl’s “In the Basement” was a fiction film about what is certainly the most notorious criminal case in recent Austrian history. But the project stretches further back—to the research and then shooting phases of “Dog Days” (2001), when Seidl observed that his fellow citizens actually live below the earth—in the underground. Everything that happens or is played out aboveground is a mix of theater and the museum of normative life, in which we do and display what “society” expects of us. If anything belowground shifts, things soon also look different in the kitchen, bathroom, living room and bedroom. According to how the basement is furnished, the activities in those rooms are quickly reorganized. You get the feeling of plates and cups fresh out of the dishwasher that look as if they have been coated with disinfectant rather than actually cleaned.

So
to
indulge those sides of ourselves that don’t coincide with what is considered acceptable by mainstream society, we have to go somewhere else, to a place where others can’t easily penetrate. It isn’t that our ground-floor existence is pure self-deception; but that it is simply stripped of all contradiction. Everything that doesn’t fit in there—the junk in our hearts and minds—is shunted below; strange monuments to obsessions and passions are thus given form. Something is common to / communicated in both spheres: Above, how well we function; below, that we don’t have to. This is how a good subject presents him- or herself. She or he has her/himself well in control, is so self-determined, that she/he knows how to find a form for every whim and every fear and every psychological wound, not to say wasteland.

But
is
it in fact good—that is, meaningful—when there is one structure for everything, one image, one figure, one gesture, one scene? And who has the upper hand there anyway? When we exert control over ourselves to our very depths, have we not in fact internalized social norms, reduced identity to idiosyncrasy, to a surplus or even byproduct that can be exchanged or jettisoned according to need?

Which
of
the figures in "In the Basement" stays with you longer is probably a question of your inner makeup, though it's hard to imagine anyone not being haunted by the woman with the baby doll: Children locked up in basements invariably come to mind when thinking about underground spaces. Such spaces seem to demand human sacrifice; and most precious of all and beloved of the gods are the innocent. Again and again this nameless woman in late middle-age goes down to a basement and takes out from some dusty, tightly stacked box one or another absolutely lifelike baby doll that she talks to, cuddles and rocks in her arms, speaking of a daddy we never see because he is, as she explains while standing in front of a world map, somewhere out there. The first trip downstairs is long, very long; she appears to live in an apartment building on one of the upper floors, one person among many. This woman lives somewhere in Austria, but it is not she whom we see in Ulrich Seidl's film. Everyone who appears here—whether as a main character or as someone merely expanding the cosmos in a short interlude—is an actor; most, but not all, are enacting their own lives.

And
"In
the Basement" takes off with a performance: In a vaulted concrete room, at the shooting range that has been installed there, an unassuming man with a surprisingly beautiful voice begins belting out Italian melodies between motionless, hanging targets. According to the credits his name is Fritz Lang—a lovely coincidence, as the film director of the same name was of course fascinated with everything that takes place underground, below the earth: those networks, organizational forms and systems that, hidden from the view of the masses, either plunge society into chaos—or rescue us from it.

That shot combines everything that will be at stake in the first half of "In the Basement": men and death. The only woman who until the stroke of the fortieth minute plays a substantial role, who is allowed a certain place, is the one with the baby doll. The child to whom she talks must be—thus contextualized—either dead, or was never born in the first place.

Music
on
the other hand runs through the entire film. Bel canto is celebrated, as are music for brass bands, pop hits and also briefly punk rock—though all this is a male realm. None of the women focused on in the film's second half listens to or makes music.

A
singer
and a tuba player are at the center of the first forty minutes. The former is Fritz Lang. When he isn't singing, we see him shooting or teaching others how to shoot—or at least the proper behavior at his shooting range. Lang fires

handguns and hunting weapons at everything that appears on his video simulator, from cardboard targets in the shape of people to moving images of animals and criminals. He has quickly taken aim and fired at so many images that, by now, he probably only perceives a vague movement, and not a picture. Lang has found his rhythm. More than any of his other shooting buddies—of which there are several "In the Basement"—he seems to be entirely comfortable with himself.

The tuba is played by Josef Ochs, who by his own admission has repeatedly been visited at home by the police. In one scene he grumbles about how government officials responsible for protecting the constitution—he calls them the Gestapo because he can't remember what they're called in the Second Republic—frequently pester him about repeat offenses—for he does have a record. Ochs makes no attempt to hide his sympathies. The cozy den in his basement is crammed full with original paintings or reproductions of the Führer and Nazi soldiers, and with daggers, bayonets, flags with swastikas, military medals, etcetera. Amongst them stand male mannequins dressed in appropriate uniforms as well as exaggeratedly sexy female mannequins, one of which Ochs has, for instance, clothed in a summer dress, with a paper boat on her head. We can survey the room at leisure in a scene in which Ochs struts about as he plays "Es zittern die morschen Knochen" (The rotten bones are trembling), the official song of the Hitler Youth. His fellow musicians from the brass band also appear very comfortable in these surroundings, as we later see. Even the neighbors, he says, like to drop by and relax and make themselves at home.

Ochs is fascinated by Führer and redeemer figures in general. He is first introduced as an admirer of Ludwig II. Portraits of the "Mad King" of Bavaria adorn an entire wall of his garage and hang in other spots as well. Ochs loves Jesus, too. Several other (though fewer) prominent spots in his convoluted basement setup are decorated with His Passion and Resurrection. Does Ochs see his comfy den as his own personal Neuschwanstein castle? Like Lang, Ochs is drawn to transgression—at one point he plays the international pop hit "Seeman (deine Heimat ist das Meer)" (Sailor, the sea is your home). Strangely affecting is a scene where he uses a bright feather duster to clean his mannequins, thereby engaging in a task that is classically and paternalistically connoted as female.

The
first
part of the film closes with Lang's song of praise for man as the crowning glory of creation. The second part, which deals with women and love, opens with a burly man who apparently works as a guard or caretaker in a (music?) theater. After that we see him in his private life: as a love slave—doing housework or in the basement as an object of torture. His wonderfully articulate and thoughtful mistress can do with him as she pleases, and she does. This abrupt transition from Lang's verses to a man who (no doubt happily) allows himself to be dominated has an ironic humor in view of all the stairs and ramps that expose the flowing passage between the theater parterre and the basement world: Social boundaries may be elastic—those between the sexes, on the other hand, are etched as if by a scalpel in the skin of reality, leaving gaping wounds. Significant is, how much in the end death and love always resemble each other and require similar poses. The man watching behind glass his majestic snake devour its prey adopts the same posture of devout humility as the love slave on all fours waiting opposite the toilet to be allowed to lick his mistress clean after she finishes peeing.

The men of the first half of the film have as counterparts in the second half three red-headed, pleasantly articulate women not identified by name: the above-mentioned sadist; a shy masochist, who turns out to have been the repeated victim of violence in human relationships and who now, working for the Catholic charity Caritas, helps woman in similar situations; and a somewhat younger, friendly and self-assured prostitute who prefers having sex for money to being treated like shit at a supermarket cash register and who appears to be ready for pretty much anything that her current job may throw at her. Like the wife of the old Indian chief in the second verse of "Da sprach der alte Häuptling der Indianer" (Then spoke the old Indian chief), they too would wrest the battle axe away from their husbands if necessary. Each of these women has a man dedicated to her, a man who is depicted solely in terms of his relationship to her and who exists exclusively for her and through her and because of her. When, in one of the interludes, the shot of a basement full of teenagers briefly appears, we see at first the sole young girl among the boys. The men in the first half, on the other hand, either had no women who felt attached to them, or largely hid them from the camera—which retrospectively sheds a note of edgy mockery on the gun enthusiasts' Islamophobic rants.

Everything that can be said about the co-existence of the gender roles is here concentrated on sex, which is tied to violence and forms of subservience throughout. That those who let themselves be hung by the scrotum or beaten on the behind desire precisely that changes nothing. It is strange, but whatever their differences, the various sex chambers are furnished much more austerely than most of the other rooms we see, the apotheoses of mass-market kitsch. They appear like transit rooms; places where no one stays—in keeping with the fleetingness of fucking.

The last image shows the prostitute squirming on all fours in a far too cramped cage. That is the film's arc: from Lang's broad gesturing in a bright, open space to captivity in a red-tinged darkness.

Good morning, darling! Good morning, time to get up! Mommy's here! Mommy's always with you. Mommy always comes. My little mouse, my sweetheart. I'm so happy that I have you.

BANANAS
PEGINA
Dole

RÖMER STAR RISER
PREMIUM
secura

The Basement as Foundation

Franz Schuh

Police investigators surmise that the 86-year-old and his grandson first cleaned up the party room and then, before rigor mortis set in, placed Mario, his arms crossed and torso bent forward, in a black garbage bag...

"Taxi für eine Leiche" (Taxi for a Corpse),
in: *News*, No. 28/2014, July 10, 2014

A productive approach to Ulrich Seidl's films is in my view offered by the kind of portraits of people we see every day: In our society heroic portraits enjoy semi-official status. In them, everyone appears to be master of himself, is economically a subject who manages his own affairs, and in terms of his economy of desire too, the person so portrayed may be regarded as being in control. His genitals never gain control over his head; he always has himself in hand.

I am not suggesting that these propaganda pictures, which are intended to impose an image of "normalcy," are exclusively lies. It is just that such semi-official portraits verge on the utopic. And since they propose this utopia—deemed desirable by certain segments of society—as a reality, it is an artist's duty to polemicize against them.

This type of polemic does not require extraordinary theoretical effort by the artist. Its strength derives from its making visible how people—if not all, then at least some—*also* are. That is, they are also unattractive beings enslaved to obsessions.

This is at least in part because between people's pursuit of happiness and the fulfillment thereof, obstacles (both individual and social) arise, invariably warping those same people. But at the same time such warping is inevitable. The happy are indeed few and far between, especially in Austria.

If this is true, and I believe it is, we must acknowledge that so-called perversions are to a large extent normal. And this normalcy, which, like every other normalcy, can veer into the horrific (the criminal, for instance), is revealed to me by Seidl's films. Consequently, it would never occur to me that this artist might be putting individual people on display as marginals to make them appear contemptible.

His films are about "truth" in the tradition of the ancient philosophical question: "What is man?" And: What do economic and political conditions make of people who, in Seidl's Film "Import Export," for instance, ruthlessly exploit the social inequalities of the world, although—or because—they themselves are poor bastards?

The intensity of Seidl's films derives in my view not least from the artist's posing age-old philosophical questions within the framework of an equally venerable philosophical tradition: If God is dead, what will become of man? The signs of the disintegration of religion, indeed the smell of decomposing faith (from which, the sexual, for instance, emanates hopelessly) are once more and once less Seidl's themes.

His material is "sensational"—first because it communicatively shines a light on things that are shrouded in silence, and second because it works through strong sensory impressions. I believe that one of Seidl's aesthetic strategies is to erase the boundary between sensationalistic marketing (for example, through exhibited sexuality) and the thorough exploration of a phenomenon.

In speaking of "erasing" I most definitely do not mean "obscuring." That, given the dominant economy of attention, the distinction is now largely academic is not the fault of the artist, even when the eradicated difference makes things easier from an artistic point of view: That way you don't have to worry about such "old" differences anymore and can artistically get right to the point.

"In the Basement" artistically erases another boundary: the one between authenticity and fiction. We cannot determine if the actors are "real" people or characters in a screenplay, simply because here (unlike in television) it does not matter. The woman who goes into her basement and takes down off her shelves boxes containing lifelike baby dolls on whom she dotes with tender maternal feelings—does she really exist?

It is unimportant, for in Seidl's staged authenticity, this woman stands for something that really does exist, that is, for absolute loneliness. In its lexical sense "absolute" means removed from, isolated—and the film shows how, in isolation, we make do with a substitute, and how substitute satisfaction, in its ghostly unreality, really does provide happiness.

In an interview with the Austrian daily "Die Presse", Ulrich Seidl offered a very precise approach to his film "In the Basement": "At one point I realized," the director said, "that in most single-family homes the basement is furnished more elaborately than the above-ground living areas. And that in their free time people go to the basement to do whatever they want to do—from sports or handicrafts to taking a sauna or having a drink with others. But now, because of certain recent crimes, the basement has taken on an entirely new meaning that has become etched into our minds and won't go away. The basement is, from earliest childhood, a place associated with darkness and fear: torture, crime, killing. That's the subject. In my film I show episodically what people do in the basement."

For me, the problem starts already with "the house." It has always been a fortress, a structure to retreat to and attack from. It offers partial protection from whatever may emerge from the forest or even the jungle of the big city. But what goes on in the house itself? "My home is my castle"—the saying always struck me as a horrible threat. In some homes the bourgeois separation of "private" and "public" (despite the inherent benefits) allows the man of the house to do what he wants. The tyrant has set up a homey place; he's the household tyrant.

In the home there is often a reigning dialectical tension that dissipates only in the basement. It is the dialectic between the publicly accessible and what for private reasons remains cloistered. In Seidl's film we see a procession of people who come alive in the basement. Most of them, to channel Goethe, have a "Here, I am a human, here it's allowed"-pathos when underground. In the basement, the home's occupants enjoy and experience freedom from society's constraints. Here at last they can indulge in their ersatz satisfactions and their compulsive obsessions.

In

"In

the Basement", Seidl's aesthetic strategy—his art of putting to effective use sensory impressions—works through something akin to moving postcard pictures—though they frequently morph into "wanted" posters. Overcome with emotion, for example, the practicing National Socialist recalls how he wanted nothing more than to take his wedding gift, a portrait of the Führer, straight into his basement and hang it on the wall. The man is a repeat offender returning to his favorite occupations—if only in the basement. Such activities are punishable by law, but this is precisely the function of the basement: to allow us to go unpunished for what is in fact criminal.

For these people the basement is the foundation of their existence. Fritzl's "real" life was not upstairs, but rather down in the basement. But his basement was hidden from the gaze of others. Seidl's film reveals the hidden to viewers. Film cannot do otherwise. This film thus creates a classic artistic tension: We are clearly shown what is normally just as clearly withheld from our gaze. Which is why it takes place in the basement. To use a metaphor drawn from the stage: We get a glimpse behind the scenes.

At no time does the practicing National Socialist come across as unlikeable. In my estimation the man belongs to the (Austrian) faction best categorized as *gemütlich* (pleasant). He plays a brass instrument—the tuba, I believe—in a traditional band. When talk turns existential he even speaks in free verse, that is, almost in poetry: "I do like my drink. / It goes hand in hand with playing. / It's a given. / Before the morning break, three spritzers / just so I can talk. / Then, with the morning break drink, ten spritzers. / And afterwards perhaps / a few shots / because everything's gone so well."

He is a lush, like you and me. He represents a magnificent, perfect cycle of addiction: First he drinks because he's worried he may not be able to play the tuba properly, then —while he's playing—he keeps his alcohol level as high as necessary, and, afterwards, since with his talent he always plays well, he gets a few shots as reward.

So the practicing National Socialist is also a fun-loving musician. He acknowledges, almost self-critically, "I'm predisposed, because my whole family drinks." For me there is no doubt: He and those like him are not outsiders here in Austria. He has the mindset on which the popular show on public TV "Musikantenstadl" (Musician's City) can always depend.

"They

go

to the basement to laugh" is how we describe people who don't want others to see how well they are doing. In Seidl's film one man goes to the basement to sing. At first I thought he was doing a send-up of an opera singer: He mocks operatic gestures, sings off-key. Or so I thought—but not in the least!

On camera the man enumerates all the operatic roles that he would be more than suited for and would still be singing today if he'd ever really been interested in doing so.

This man—an outsider, a dilettante glutton for ridicule? Not at all! In the arts world, overestimating your talent is normal and, like the middle-aged woman who, with her beloved baby dolls, embodies total solitude and a hollowed-out love for artificial people, so we see in the singer the hubris that is so often found in the arts.

System-
atizing
crudely, we allow that the basement mirrors the state and the society: maternal love, a nucleus of the state; the institution of an art without standards, an artistic drive going through the motions that operates on conceit; the political obscenity that, feigning populism, makes deadly claims on power; and last but not least a sexuality that has to be staged in order for desire to transpire: "When I want to be really dominant, I take him to the basement." The foundation of which is: "I absolutely adore my love slave. And the opposite is also true."

Strange. If you look closely, as Seidl does with his camera, you cannot but recognize—precisely via a sexual practice based on the pathos of power and subjugation—how incredibly pitiful it all is.

But the pathos derives not from the masochistic subjugation, but rather from the contortions some people must engage in to feel desire. Still, pity for an overworked horniness is a taboo in a society in which many have to live off pornography.

That said, Seidl's images of basement sex are antipornographic. "You know how much I love to hoist you by the balls," says the woman, and the viewer's gaze falls on a penis tied by a rope. It is then hoisted up—which only highlights the fact that the absolute ridiculousness of the penis was apparent from the beginning.

I've never eaten baboon, but I've tasted every other animal.

When the horn sounds the hunt,
And mama feels an itch in front,
And papa grows a hard-on,
Spring will soon warm the garden.

FCK
THT
SHT
neuruppin

FreQuency

Basements, Tunnels, Secret Rooms

Ute Woltron

Hasn't modern society long since led to a civilized wilderness to which man reacts like a Neanderthal?

Friedrich Dürrenmatt

Before *Homo domesticus*—builder-humans—entered the scene, our ancestors, as we all know, lived in caves. Caves offered protection from the elements, enemies and wild beasts; they were a stone-walled refuge from the tribulations and dangers that lurked outside on open ground.

Since then of course architecture and construction have come a long way, but the original protective function already present in the cave has survived. The human desire for a safe enclosure in which we, alone or with our tribe, can be ourselves, unseen and undisturbed, is very much alive. Architecture, its practitioners like to say, is our third skin; it envelops us like our garments. Our built environment significantly determines our well-being. Depending on its form and the intentions of its designers, a structure can be open, embracing the outside, or closed-in like a bunker—completely turned toward the interior.

For most of human history, until the advent of cities, the world's common mortals usually erected their own dwellings, building huts and houses with their own hands and as they saw fit. In 1900 only 10 percent of the world's population lived in cities. Today more than 50 percent do. With the invention of the apartment building and rental flat, modern man has once again become a nomad. He occupies what might be called a prefabricated residential cave that he can change almost like clothing. Somehow that isn't always enough, however; somehow many of us appear to crave a kind of cave in which we can act bizarre and be undisturbed: a basement! What, apart from a basement, offers such absolute seclusion and refuge?

Architectural history provides many examples of the human longing for a safe, enclosed and often secret room. Among the earliest such spaces were the countless hidden chambers inside and even underneath Egyptian pyramids. They were intended to thwart grave robbers and other intruders and serve for all eternity as a dwelling for the transforming immortal Ba soul of the deceased. Aztec pyramids and temples of Central America also had concealed basements and secret rooms, while most other sacred buildings comprise an innermost sanctum that is almost invariably windowless. From the Latin *cella*—the "little room" at the center of Greek and Roman temples that housed the statues of the divinities—we inherited the concept and word "cellar."

The original cellar was a closed-off, hidden and windowless room that sheltered a secret. Only a select group of the chosen were allowed ingress; the general public was excluded. For the latter, outside the temple, altars were erected where official rituals were performed—the altar being in some ways an accessible façade before the inaccessible, concealed Holy of Holies.

Subsequently, not only the sacred, but also the forbidden retreated underground. The persecuted Christians of Rome met in catacombs and basements. During the reign of Elizabeth I in England, when, after 1558, Catholic priests risked life imprisonment for performing their offices, they would hide in so-called priest holes if authorities came looking for them. These hiding places can still be found in many castles in Britain—cells concealed in walls, small underground rooms behind double paneling and invisible entrances. Of course holocaust hiding places, often walled off in basements, also belong to this tragic category of secret room. And let us not forget that at one time or another during the bombings of World War II, half of Europe's population huddled in underground air-raid shelters. Contrast those structures with the bunkers of power. In Bucharest, Nicolae Ceauşescu's Securitate dug a secret network of underground tunnels that linked arsenals and command centers. Hitler's personal quarters in the Congress Hall on the Nazi party rally grounds in Nuremberg were immense, windowless and stone-walled basement rooms. And though Saddam Hussein was not exactly there by choice, he spent several months in a cramped Iraqi cellar before he was captured.

And
then
there is the harmless traditional earthen cellar that once was part of all farmhouses. Because of its constant temperature and humidity, it served for storing food. Winter apples, carrots and sauerkraut survived the winter there, while in summer vinegar, cider and wine were kept suitably cool. Of course before the invention of modern machinery, cellars were laboriously dug out and flattened by hand to create the bare floor that allowed for contact between air and soil, resulting in the special basement climate. Accordingly, these cellars were small and highly prized.

It was not only in the countryside that people excavated beneath their houses. All of Vienna, for example, is criss-crossed by a little-known basement landscape that often extends several stories below ground. At the bottom level are former ice cellars where blocks of ice that had been cut in the winter were kept on straw and used for refrigeration till the next freeze. Since the 1930s, and the advent of refrigerators, these ice cellars have usually sat vacant. But earth cellars are enjoying a renaissance; today's builders often include an uninsulated cellar in new homes so that eager gardeners have space to store the fruits of their labor.

The (in)famous basement den, where you can do everything that is forbidden in the spic'n-span upstairs living quarters—smoking, drinking, partying, being loud—is in fact a recent invention. It was not until the 1960s that builders of single-family dwellings were able to affordably excavate and seal basements and so provide new homeowners with useable underground rooms.

Most passers-by would never guess, but many of those small sheds at community garden allotments around Vienna have a secret of their own: They sit atop an often large, underground extension. The sheds are subject to tight surface area and height restrictions. Some people merely circumvent the rules and excavate below their entire plot to gain additional useable space. Those cute little cottages in green spaces thus become the acme of well-concealed and of course subversive and unlawful underground constructions.

But official Austria has another assortment of basements and tunnels to contend with; some are several centuries old, while others, such as POW or labor camps or underground airplane hangars, are from the Nazi period. These cavernous subterranean galleries stretch for several hundred kilometers across the entire "underground republic." Where exactly the vast galleries are found, no one likes to say. Few of the people who happen to walk a few meters above them have any idea that they are there. As recently as a couple of decades ago, entire single-family-home developments were constructed over these networks of galleries, without the people who bought the land and built their houses above them even suspecting their presence.

Indeed,
people
are always digging unfathomable constructions below the earth. Governments and individuals alike are motivated to do so. William Cavendish-Scott-Bentinck, for instance, the 5th Duke of Portland, for reasons that he took with him to the grave, decided in 1854 to avoid thereafter every form of human contact. To that end he had an extensive warren of rooms excavated beneath and around Welbeck Abbey, his enormous, historic estate in England's Nottinghamshire. This network comprised a library and a ballroom for 2000 people, in which of course no one ever danced. A 25-kilometer-long network of tunnels connected his peculiar basement abode with the stables and even the train station in the closest village. The passages were so capacious that the eccentric duke could travel by carriage to his private railway car while hidden from anyone's view. He communicated with his servants by means of two mailboxes, one for incoming, the other for outgoing messages.

In Chicago in the 1880s, Herman Webster Mudgett, better known as Dr. Henry Howard Holmes, and one of the first mass murderers ever convicted in North America, had a labyrinthine hotel erected. He purposely changed builders on a routine basis, so that no single person would have even a glimpse of the building's entire layout. Holmes's plans, you see, called for innumerable secret cellars—sealed and sound-proof rooms—for murdering guests and employees. He is reckoned to have killed some two hundred people, whose life insurance he pocketed and whose mortal remains he sold off to a nearby faculty of medicine. In 1896 he was found guilty for his crimes and hanged. The building, which came to be known as "Murder Castle", burned to the ground in 1895.

But basements can also harbor more convivial, though still illegal, activities, as some construction workers discovered in New York in 2007 while renovating an old coffee-house. They uncovered a secret door that led to a concealed underground establishment where, in the 1920s, when alcohol was considered "the devil's drink" and banned, people congregated to defy Prohibition. These illegal basement bars, known as speakeasies or blind pigs, numbered in the hundreds. Beneath the foundations of ostensibly aboveboard businesses, entire casinos, bars and ballrooms were in operation. One such storied Prohibition establishment was New York City's 21 Club, whose entrance was a secret door disguised as a massive concrete wall.

In the USA, secret and ultra-secure basement rooms are again in high demand, in the form of panic rooms. These are intended to protect affluent clients from burglars, just as priest holes of yore protected England's Catholic clergy from authorities: *Sic transit gloria mundi*. That may have crossed the minds of the monks at the Mont Sainte-Odile monastery in France where, between August 2000 and May 2002, some 1100 precious books disappeared one after another from their library, even though the latter was not open to the public. What even they did not know, but what the thief who was later caught thanks to a CCTV camera had discovered was that there was a secret room in the monastery walls from which a sophisticated mechanism allowed one of the bookshelves to be pushed aside, granting clandestine access to the library. The otherwise upstanding book thief had learned about the secret from an old, forgotten plan of the monastery that he had chanced upon in a municipal archive.

In closing, each of us may ask ourselves the question: Does the basement make the secret, or does the secret construct the basement? Which of us cavemen can answer this question with certainty?

I do like my drink. It goes hand in hand with playing. It's a given. Before the morning break, three spritzers just so I can talk. Then, with the morning break drink, ten spritzers. And afterwards perhaps a few shots, because everything's gone so well. But I'm predisposed, because my whole family drinks.

That Hitler portrait behind me,
I got it for my wedding. I wanted
to go right home and hang it up
in the basement. It was the most
wonderful wedding gift I got.

Lived Underworld

Herbert Lachmayer

In German, when you say that someone is "in the basement," you are usually referring not to a physical location, but to the fragile mood that the person is in. H.C. Artmann's "Köllastiagn" (Viennese for basement stairway)—a poem from his book "med ana schwoazzn dintn" (With Black Ink)—evinces macabre details, awakening fears that escalate in the poet's verses. Fear and the macabre may be natural residents of the basement, even when you carry them within you: when you think of a basement, or are in one and haven't yet left it. The basement has always been synonymous with the hidden, the bizarre, the buried—and at the same time a sign of a sanctum which, protected by subterranean seclusion, can fulfill its own mythological temporality. Attentiveness to the highest ambivalence is in order when you literally go "below daylight." When you are on the "Köllastiagn" your individuality is tested by fear. Underground spaces have an anonymizing effect and give rise to the alluring feeling of "passionate self-dissolution"—even though you know it's going to hurt. This threatening-pleasurable feeling of ego dissolution corresponds to the psychological realm of the unconscious in therapy. To accept that, to expose yourself to unimaginable surprises, liberates the field of unresolved tension between protective measures (rationalization) and a certain abandon. You are submitting yourself to the pull of the awaiting absorption—and neither aspect of this paradoxical suspension of consciousness provides a solution. The choice of one or the other no longer functions properly.

If, "whistling in the woods" or mouthing words of comfort to yourself, you attempt to sneak into one or another recess in that spooky realm and hide there to make yourself inconspicuous, you achieve the opposite: For precisely this seemingly protective recess reveals itself to be the possible hiding place of a young basilisk whose very gaze will bring about your downfall. So, too, in Ulrich Seidl's film: Fear and lust oscillate in this ambiguity as much as do brutal pain and feelings of arousal and well-being; it is simply that the objects of desire have not yet revealed themselves. The palette of emotional clichés is familiar: Your heart is in your mouth, your breathing is labored, you think you hear sounds that demand immediate interpretation, you have butterflies in your stomach. Naturally lighting is decisive here—no sooner do you flick on the fickle basement light than you begin to fantasize about it suddenly plunging you back into darkness.

Only
St Monica,
the mother of Augustine, was vouchsafed the right to develop an unambivalent relationship to the basement; as a young girl she had to fetch wine from the cellar—and so at a tender age apparently developed a taste for that basement beverage. This pleasant experience led her to view the basement as an unequivocal haven of pleasure. On the other hand Piranesi, in his "Carceri," reveals to us basement systems of unsuspected gloom and menace. They are places where amphorae, that for eons have held no water, let alone wine, provide the decaying evidence of an earlier life—a solitary melancholy genius loci leans his elbows against the clay vessels that no longer afford any consolation. Endless staircases, whose bewildering directions may bring Escher to mind, reveal the redundancy of an infinity that must be managed

Giovanni Battista Piranesi, "Carceri," plate 14, 1750, etching, 15 × 53 cm

by finite, if futile, Sisyphus-like feats of movement which you feel too weak to muster. In Seidl's film, however, the basement is a place of sensual ecstasy—as soon as you are caught in the pull of the ritual, a previously unknown, autonomous momentum sets in, imposing its own bizarre rules, necessary and absolute, yet promising something that life at street level usually no longer presents: heightened intensity of experience, true devotion borne of desperation, bizarre lust and the

M.C. Escher, "Relativity," 1953, lithograph, 27,7 × 29,2 cm

profane self-transcendence of being allowed to be "outside yourself." Basements communicate a "dense vacuum" in which nothing but the air from above offers a vital connection with the outer world. In the basement, unacknowledged and forbidden desires can be manifested; threats from society seem to be eliminated—except for the companions taken along to participate in the routine magical ritual. In the basement, the "15 minutes of truth" can transpire undisturbed; orphic streams of words—here with Viennese accents—reveal an ever new "underlying" authenticity. This is what Ulrich Seidl's protagonists express. One scene has viewers accompany a woman into the basement. The way she locks the door from inside may arouse in us a feeling of hermetic finality. With touching tenderness she takes a lifelike latex infant from a shoebox and begins her motherly (or grandmotherly?) acts of love and nurturing. We follow the performance spellbound and may realize with horror that the inanimate and unresponsive doll stimulates the woman to an unrelenting flow of signs of love. The film however is not a documentary, but a staging which, though often composed like a painting, still manages to conceal its director's intervention. We encounter what remains as a "given." This power, as a director working with non-professional actors, to elicit emotions, to let them occur and what's more to capture them on film distinguishes Seidl as a go-between on the frontier, a man familiar with obsessions. On the one hand he is able to allow his actors an inner mental state in all its obsessiveness. And on the other hand he succeeds in capturing these highly individualized stories of desire in a medium that enables viewers to voyeuristically share in this object of fascination. Fascination is always both the disgust for the object that we find completely repellent and at the same time the enormous attraction that the "other face" of the object triggers in us.

In the episode with the sadomasochistic couple the basement extends to encompass the entire house and the actual basement retains a special status as a "chamber of terror." While the humiliations in the bathroom, living room or staircase often display athletic ambitions, the basement has the privilege of literally accommodating the polymorphic diversity of new ideas and hype, of being a place of inspiration. Here again we may invoke Piranesi, whose substructures show the external façades of basements that from deep down push up over the earth's surface while, at the same time, allowing us a glimpse of underlying, deeper cellar systems. In the case of the well-known sexual offender from Amstetten, Josef Fritzl, the horror also occurred in the basement; climbing back up to the ground floor we seemingly reach the world of middle-class order—which was for years the only thing Fritzl's neighbors noticed. Above ground the regularity of accepted

The Palazzo Orsini (16th century) showing ancient substructures of the Teatro Marcello

norms appeared to hold sway—but only as a mask, a calculated and rehearsed illusion intended for the exterior, a magic cap of invisibility that, in retrospect, left the "normal people" of the neighborhood stunned not only by the abysses that opened up in their neighbor's "soul," but by the realization that the actual, physical basement of this house of lust and torture served as a place for the release of authoritarian notions of pleasure.

"Today the basement is ours, and tomorrow the whole world"—this refrain likely inspired the film's "Nazi cell," a small retinue of sympathizers who have collected around a "lone combatant" and gather in a "party room" lovingly decorated with Nazi trophies to fantasize about a future that seeks the death of all democracies. But it also has a deeply necrophilic aspect, for in this “furnished Valhalla” of middle-class design it is not just that the cult of the past is being embraced, but also that a “drunken present” as the foundation of a new, grand “Über-Germany” is being celebrated.

Anyone
who
purports to be scandalized by Seidl’s film should be reminded how powerfully repression and buried fantasies of lust act on us—namely, as something completely and absolutely positive, for which there is no room in what remains of our liberal middle-class society that instead holds up the consumption of goods as a permanent substitute satisfaction, (which are always and de facto however the substitute for a frustration, to the exclusion of any authentic sensorial satisfaction). With his basement film the director evokes a legitimate vital experiential capacity that shows its actors to be the protagonists of libido-driven self-fulfillment—with the ultimate effect that their outraged voyeurism falls back on those doing the gawking. No matter how worked up they want to get about the ritual, their moralizing condemnation instead reveals their inability to embrace extreme desire. And thus they are left with all the rancid resentment of having paid for the pleasure of seeing a movie that in the end simply holds up a mirror to their own “compulsion to frustration.”

TROCKENANWEISUNG
1
2
3
4
5
6
WASCHANLEITUNG WESS
1
2
3
4
5
6

PMC

A man is always young and trim,
For him time stands still.
Meanwhile his wife will age—
Pointless to express outrage,
Or mourn her youth,
Or shed tears, in truth,
For what's left of her days,
As she helplessly decays.
While he, with vigor blessed,

Beats on his heroic chest,
He feels again his vigor grow,
His manhood stiffens down below.
Whenever a lass he spies,
A superman, he feels with pride.
Since ere the world began,
Its highest principle is man.

FILA

GORDON'S
LONDON DRY GIN

The Moment When You Gag on Your Laughter

Ulrich Seidl in conversation with
Markus Keuschnigg and Claus Philipp

Ulrich Seidl, what is your personal experience of basements?

The first basement that left a lasting impression on me was the basement of my childhood, my grandmother's root cellar. You had to go out of the house and cross the garden to an outbuilding where you descended the cellar steps. The padlock on the creaky door that you had to open wide in order to see anything in the dark. The cool, damp air that engulfed you, surrounded you. The musty smell of soil that mixed with the odors of the food stored in the cellar: meat, bacon, sausage and cheese. The potatoes and carrots that were covered with soil, the preserved eggs in jars, the smell of pickles, cider and elderberry syrup. The fear that the door might suddenly shut, the fear of total darkness, the fear of being locked in—those are also memories. As a boy I would be locked in my parent's basement as a punishment—which didn't happen very often and which apparently didn't do me any lasting damage.

About basements it is safe to say that almost everyone has one, almost no one will show it to you. Can you describe how you researched your film? Did you go out looking for specific basements?

In fact it was hard to gain access to people and their basements. It's easy enough to find the normal, banal, harmless. Many people are happy to show off their basement, but what you encounter is mostly hobby areas such as workshops, fitness or party rooms, or even entire basements devoted to a husband's model railway or beer coaster collection. But I was looking for abysses, and how do you go about finding them? How do you find people who have something to hide?

After several weeks of research—which mainly consisted of going door to door and knocking—the results were so frustrating that we began to concentrate on more well-known themes: guns or underground shooting ranges, for instance, and we explored the SM-scene. It was half a year before we could even begin filming, although the search for additional people and locations stretched on for a very long time. Now that it's finished, I know that "In the Basement" is a film that you could keep working on, keep filming, without ever exhausting the subject.

What truths do Austrians in particular and people in general stow away in their basement?

For Austrians the basement has a significance that may not exist in other countries. Austrians often spend their free time in their basement. Down there, they can be who they want—men, fathers, housewives, couples or children. Down there, they can indulge their needs, hobbies, passions and obsessions. The basement is a locus of free time and the private. But for many people the basement is also a place of the unconscious, a place of darkness and a place of fear. For some people that grows out of personal experience, for others a childhood memory. In fact, the basement was and is a place of hiding, a place of secret crime, a place of abuse and rape, a place of captivity, torture and violence.

The crimes of Wolfgang Priklopil and Josef Fritzl, notorious pedophiles who each kept a young girl prisoner for years or decades, have led to a distorted view elsewhere of Austria and its basements. Did that motivate you to make this film, or deter you from it?

Neither.

The idea for this film originated long before those crimes came to light. It occurred to me around the time of "Dog Days" (2001), when I was location-scouting with my crew in suburbs, exploring and criss-crossing housing developments, urban deserts, row houses and single-family-housing ghettos. The more homes I visited and the more basements I went down into, the more I realized that basement rooms are often more lavishly conceived than actual living areas, and that the inhabitants of these dwellings like their basements more than their living rooms and spend more time down there. The living room is often only for show. That was new to me, a new realization. Then, in the past few years, as we all know, Austria gained regretful worldwide notoriety for its basements. Things that you could never imagine were a reality. Austria has been stigmatized. So you have to accept the fact that, regardless of how or what my film deals with or portrays, no matter what film you make on this theme: In the minds of the audience, the crimes of Fritzl and Priklopil will always be present.

Why, after your "PARADISE" fiction trilogy, did you return to the documentary form with this film?

For me personally and for my artistic work it is, quite simply, essential that I constantly plunge back into reality. My fiction films are nourished and often inspired by this. Getting to know new people and new worlds has always been and remains very enriching. Which does not mean that it is always pleasant. You repeatedly come into contact with life and destinies, you repeatedly witness the traps that people are born, or have slid, into. Humanity never ceases to amaze me: what people put themselves through to fulfill their longings, meet their obligations, sublimate their inadequacies, act out their need for power, or repress their sexuality. Or how people fight for their dignity, a bit of affection, a modicum of happiness. Often, what I experience and witness seizes hold of me, often I close the door shaken, often I am dismayed by the images of what people do to each other, usually without bad intentions. It's normal. You sense and feel the abysses hidden there—and in the best case you sense your own abysses as well.

The film's main threads deal with people whose passions and interests are far from socially acceptable, whereas the traditional hobby basement or party basement or laundry room is represented only in vignettes. Why do you favor the extreme?

I don't. Admittedly, very few of us have a picture of Hitler hanging on our walls, but rejection and hatred of or indifference toward the Other can be found everywhere.

The socially acceptable, as you put it, is only a veneer. Beneath that is the private, the real truth, real life. If extremes form the core of the film, it is because I believe that this "extreme" in one form or another, in a modified or diluted form, applies to us all. None of us are immune to xenophobia, we all have our fears and abysses—be they fascistic sympathies, repressed tendencies to violence, unexpressed desires for power, or repression or sexual fantasies that deviate from so-called normalcy.

How else can we explain why violence and abuse in couples, families and between adults and children are so common? How else can we explain why violence and abuse, whether physical or psychological, occur in all social institutions, public and private, religious or progressive-secular in orientation? Wherever people are allowed the possibility of exercising power over others, you find oppression, humiliation, exploitation and abuse.

One could sum up your previous work with professional actors and non-professionals by saying: They are all treated equally as actors, as the inhabitants of your very precisely framed tableaux. What must an actor be able to "do" for your films?

To inhabit the tableaux, as you put it, an actor must be able to be "only" him- or herself: his facial expression, body language, gaze—these are essential. Although we frame the image to the millimeter, although we choose and arrange both the location and the space, the person looking directly at the camera is at the center. His gaze meets the spectator's gaze. And the spectator should not be able to avoid it.

In all of your films you seek out and find truths that aren't necessarily realistic. I'm referring to the much-noted integration of documentary stylistic techniques with those of fiction cinema that is at the heart of your work. To put it differently: It would not be a Seidl film if fact and fiction weren't intricately intertwined. I'm thinking for example of the scenes with the woman and the baby dolls. Could you tell us a bit more about them?

As always with my films, you set out on a journey into the unknown, into unknown places and people. You have certain ideas, you have a concept in mind—and with all that you plunge into reality. For me it's never about illustrating that reality; I instead want to discover my own view of the reality I find. Your perspective of reality is the cinematographic gaze that shapes that reality. Through it I try to show what I see, what I'm touched by, what I want to reveal to my viewers. With my cinematographic gaze I try to approach my protagonists and to gather filmic fragments of reality, none of which is complete or definitive.

The woman with the baby dolls is a good example of how, given my approach to reality, the filmic narration is sometimes invented. The woman who plays these scenes with the doll did have one of those strikingly realistic Reborn babies in her apartment, but not in the basement. The story that the film tells—namely, that this woman has several "babies" hidden in her basement that she talks to every day—is an invented story. Only the location is real. The scenes were shot in her actual basement.

It is no accident that, after "PARADISE", a book of photographs is being published to accompany "In the Basement." The photographic aspect of your tableaux appears to be increasingly important for you. What does the choice of these pictures represent for you—both for the editing of the film and the montage of this book?

Those are two different things. For the film's editing, the rule is always that every shot, every scene must serve the film's dramaturgy as a whole as well as its narrative rhythm. A scene makes it into the film only when, in terms of content, association, atmosphere and dramaturgy, its inclusion fits in to the filmic structure.

The design of a book of photographs follows other rules. Here it's about selecting individual film stills that also function as photographs. I don't need to have seen the film to view these photos; each image should be able to stand on its own independent of the film's story. And then it's a matter of juxtaposing the film images and the texts so that a tension is created—but also a unity of text and pictures.

In Austria we say about someone who has no sense of humor that he goes into the basement to laugh. You certainly cannot be accused of lacking a sense of humor. "In the Basement" is in part a strikingly funny film—and not just because some of your characters tell jokes on camera. In it the easy- and hard-to-digest go hand in hand. Do you see your films also as "human comedies"?

Humor
is
important for me in all my films, but what is new here are the obscene male jokes. They too, in a certain way, describe realities. They cloak male sexual fantasies, racism and sexism in a supposedly "humorous" guise that is socially acceptable. Often while shooting a scene I would ask myself: Should I laugh or cry? Maybe my next project should be a film about male jokes. (laughs) And as far as the human comedy is concerned: I would describe it instead as tragedy, given what and how things are shown. But it is true that I always look for the comic in the tragic, and precisely for the point when the viewer gags on his laughter.

At some point I discovered that I can shoot off a very impressive wad of semen. And if I do the famous coitus interruptus—and pull out and then shoot—the ladies are quite amazed at the load that comes out of me.

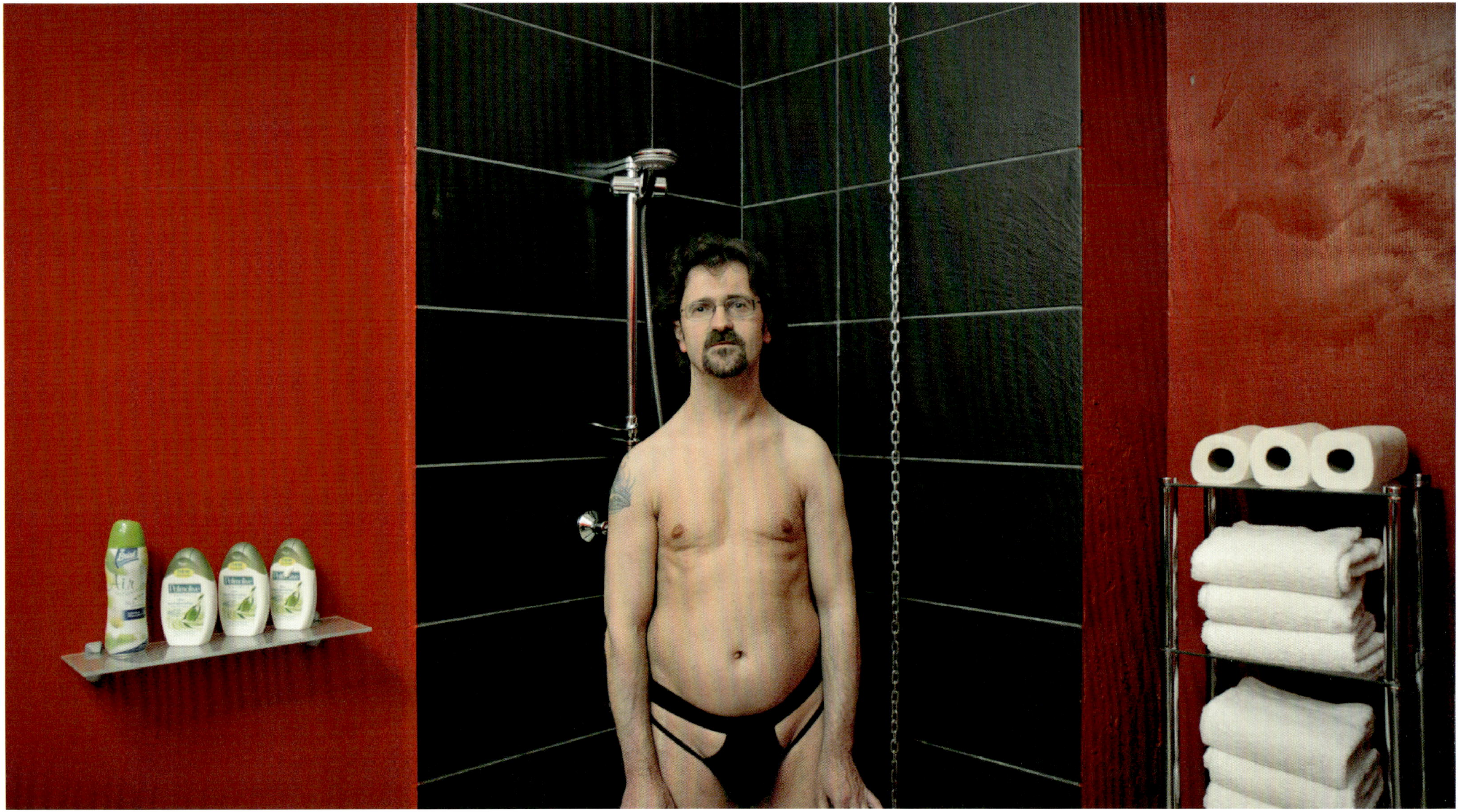

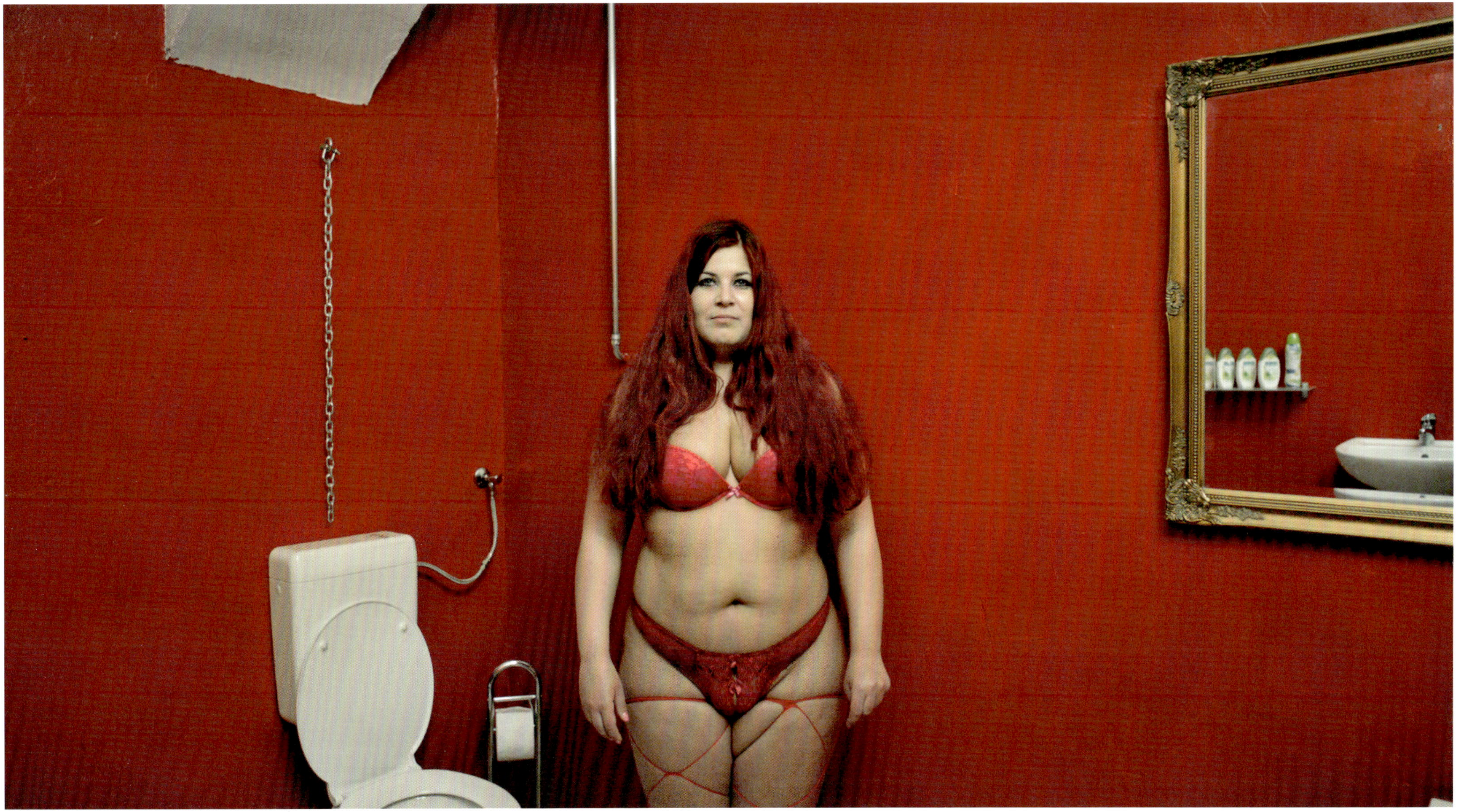

I used to be in sales. But now, I don't know. I don't like retail anymore. You have to be friendly, no matter how rude people are. So I said, I'll look around and maybe change fields.

I absolutely adore my love slave. And the opposite is also true. And when I want to be really dominant, I take him to the basement.

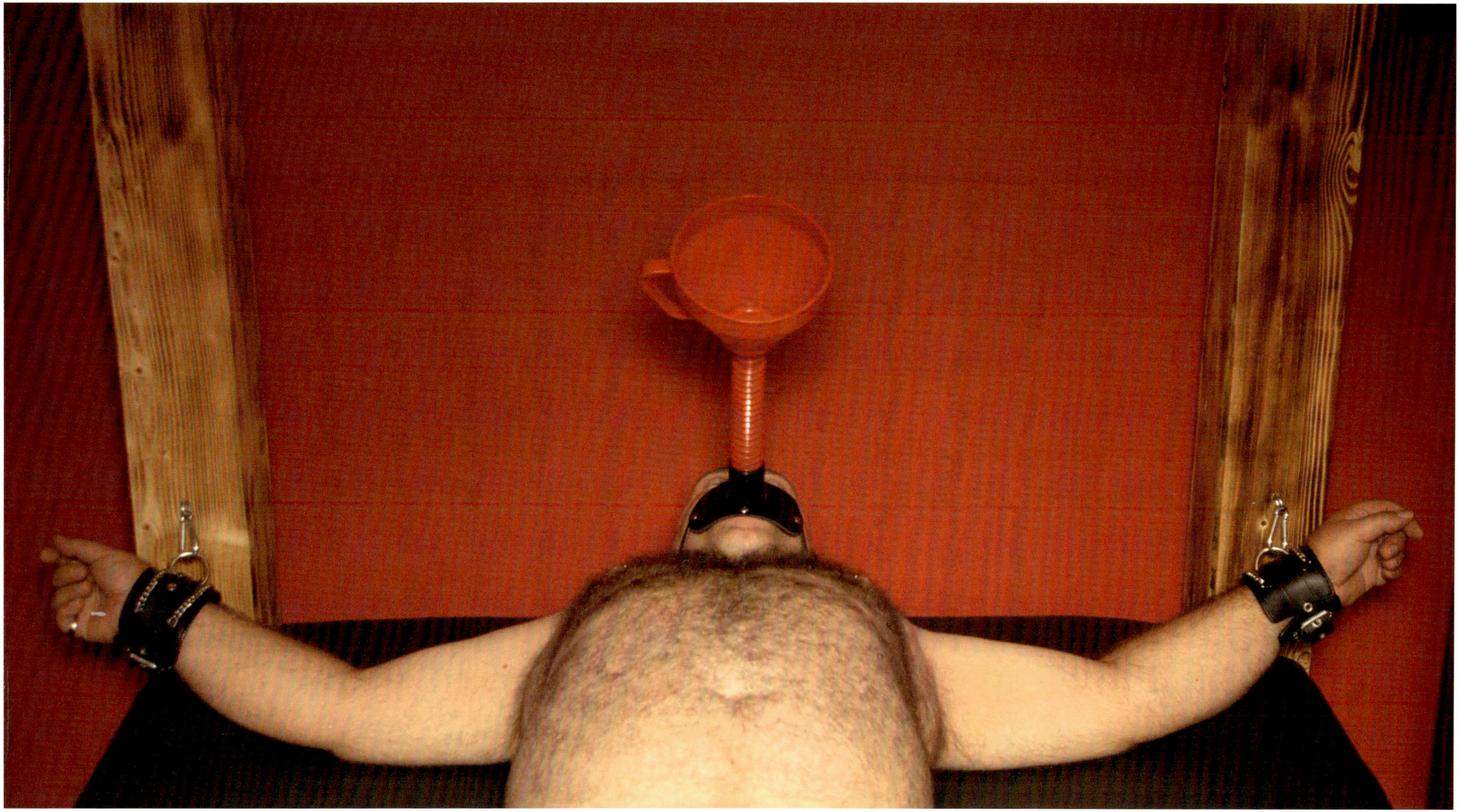

I'm a masochist. I like pain of every kind. Needles through my nipples. Needles in my back. I've had two needle corsets. I like blows of all kinds, that leave marks, or don't. Slaps. Verbal humiliation, being scolded. I can free my mind, totally let go. And simply enjoy. It's wonderful.

Someone I can do whatever I want with is, sexually, not for me. I might as well get a dog or something. When it comes to sex, the man has to be in charge.
In every way. He has to take me when he wants, where he wants.

Warthog down there doesn't have dark meat like our wild boar. Warthog meat is light, like turkey. But wonderful, and very, very tasty.

It’s my cock. It’s my scrotum. My slave’s body belongs to me. I have total control over it.

Different peoples—such as Turks and other primitive races, like Huns... When they came up here, they'd slaughter our men and take the women prisoner and enslave the children and rape the women to make it clear, "Now you belong to us. Now you are our subjects." Are you aware of that? Do you know that or not?

I realized I seem to really get along with prostitutes. Because, as funny as it may sound, they like me. I don't know why, but... with most of them I don't have to pay.

I'm the Führer...
of this party.

Appendix

Ulrich Seidl

Born in Vienna in 1952, Ulrich Seidl began his film career with documentary films such as "Good News" (1990) and "Models" (1998), which received great acclaim—and aroused just as much controversy—and won numerous international prizes. Of "Animal Love" (Tierische Liebe, 1995), Werner Herzog declared: "Never before in cinema have I been able to look straight into hell."

In 2001 Seidl was awarded the Grand Jury Prize in Venice for his episodic fiction feature "Dogdays" (Hundstage). His subsequent films have oscillated between documentary and fiction. In 2007 his second fiction feature "Import Export" premiered in competition at the Cannes film festival. It was followed by three more features over the next four years. In 2012 the first part of his "PARADISE" trilogy, "PARADISE: Love" (PARADIES: Liebe) premiered in competition in Cannes. A few months later, at the Venice film festival, Seidl was awarded a second Grand Jury Prize for "PARADISE: Faith" (PARADIES: Glaube). The final part of the trilogy, "PARADISE: Hope" (PARADIES: Hoffnung) premiered in 2013 in competition at the Berlin film festival. In 2014 Seidl unspooled his latest film "In the Basement" (Im Keller).

Ulrich Seidl has also worked twice in theater: His play "Our Father" (Vater unser) premiered at the Berlin Volksbühne in 2004, and five years later he developed and staged for the Munich Kammerspiele and the Vienna Festwoche "Bad Boys / Hideous Men" (Böse Buben / Fiese Männer), based on texts by David Foster Wallace. Seidl works and lives with the film journalist and filmmaker Veronika Franz, who since 1996 has collaborated on all his films as co-scriptwriter.

Filmography

2014	"In the Basement"
2012	"PARADISE: Hope"
2012	"PARADISE: Love"
2012	"PARADISE: Faith"
2012	"Bad Boys / Hideous Men" (stage play, Wiener Festwochen, Münchner Kammerspiele)
2007	"Import Export"
2006	"Brothers, Let Us Be Merry"
2004	"Our Father" (stage play, Volksbühne Berlin)
2003	"Jesus, You Know"
2001	"State of the Nation"
2001	"Dog Days"
1998	"Models"
1998	"Fun Without Limits" (TV)
1997	"The Bosom Friend" (TV)
1996	"Pictures at an Exhibition" (TV)
1995	"Animal Love"
1994	"The Last Men" (TV)
1992	"Losses to Be Expected"
1990	"Good News"
1984	"Look 84" (unreleased)
1982	"The Prom" (short)
1980	"One Forty" (short)

Awards (selection)

2014 “PARADISE: Love” – Austrian Film Award – Best Female Act Maria Hofstätter; 2013 “PARADISE: Love” – Vienna Film Award – Austria / Austrian Film Prize – Best Austrian Feature Film / “PARADISE: Faith” – European Sound Designer Award – European Film Academy – Berlin, Germany / Honour Prize – Molodist IFF – Kiev, Ukraine (for World Cinema Contribution) / Outstanding Achievement in the Arts Award – IFF Message To Man – St. Petersburg, Russia / Golden Apricot Special Prize Master – Yerevan IFF – Armenia / Golden Camera – art ff Trenčín – Slovakia (for Extraordinary Contribution to Cinema); 2012 “PARADISE: Faith” – Special Prize of the Jury – Venice, Italy / Best Script and Eurimages Prize (Best Coproduction) – Sevilla, Spain / Zloty Glan, Forum for European Films Cinergia – Łódź, Poland (for his Contribution to European Cinema) / Golden Honorary Prize of Lower Austria / “PARADISE: Love” – Palič Tower – Best Director – Serbia; 2011 Maverick Award – Motovun, Croatia; 2010 Bremen Film Prize – Germany; 2008 Amnesty International Award – Festival Internacional de Cinema Independente – Lisbon, Portugal; 2007 “Import Export” – Golden Apricot – Yerevan IFF – Armenia / Palič Tower – Serbia / Main Prize – Bangkok, Thailand; 2005 Film Prize of Lower Austria – Austria; 2004 Best Director – Riga, Latvia; 2003 IFF – Gijón, Spain (for the intensive search for the boundaries between reality and fiction in contemporary cinema) / “Jesus, You Know” – Best Documentary – Karlovy Vary, Czech Republic / Film Prize – Viennale – Vienna, Austria / Prize of the Association québécoise des critiques – Montréal, Canada; 2002 “Dog Days” – Special Award of the Jury – Oporto IFF – Portugal / Honorary Prize of the Federal Chancellory – Austria; 2001 “Dog Days” – Silver Lion – Venice, Italy / Best Film, Best Director – Bratislava, Slovakia / Best Film – IFF – Gijón, Spain / FIPRESCI Prize for Discovery of the Year / Most Successful Austrian Feature Film for the Year 2001/2002 – Austria / “Models” – Best Feature Film – Television Prize – Austria; 2000 “Models” – Audience Award – Sarajevo, Bosnia-Herzegovina; 1999 Silver Venus (Advertising Campaign Schwarzseher ORF); 1996 “Animal Love” – Best Documentary – Potsdam, Germany; 1992 “Losses to Be Expected” – Runner-up Prize – Yamagata, Japan / Jury Prize – Amsterdam, The Netherlands / Austrian Film Days Prize – Austria; 1991 “Good News” – Prix des bibliothèques – Paris, France / Vienna Film Prize – Austria

Biographies

Authors

Olaf Möller: from Cologne. Writes about and shows films. He has contributed to numerous publications on the life and work of such directors as Romuald Karmakar, Dominik Graf, Michael Pilz, John Cook and Mansur Madavi.

Franz Schuh, PhD, born on March 15, 1947, lives as a writer and critic in Vienna. He is a lecturer at the University of Applied Arts and the Reinhardt Seminar. He is a freelance contributor to the weekly newspaper "Die Zeit". His most recent books: "Der Krückenkaktus" (2011), "Sämtliche Leidenschaften" (2014).

Ute Woltron studied architecture and lives as a journalist and author in Vienna and Lower Austria. She has published in such magazines and newspapers as "trend", "profil", "der Standard" and "Die Presse", and produced shows on cultural matters for Radio Ö1, among others.

Herbert Lachmayer was born in 1948 and is a cultural philosopher and curator. A professor at the University of Fine Arts in Linz in the Staging Knowledge department, he is also the director of the DA PONTE Research Center in Vienna.

Markus Keuschnigg was born in 1981 in the Tirol and works as a freelance film critic for Radio FM4, Radio Ö1 and the daily newspapers "Die Presse". In 2010 he and some friends founded the /slash Film Festival, Austria's first fantastic film festival, of which he has been the artistic director ever since.

Editors

Claus Philipp, born in Wels in Upper Austria in 1966, lives in Vienna where he is an arts journalist and manager of Stadtkino film distribution. Together with Astrid Wolfig he recently edited a book of photographs and essays on Ulrich Seidl's "PARADISE" trilogy. He has also published works on such directors as Alexander Kluge and Christoph Schlingensief.

Astrid Wolfig studied Media and Communications Design in Salzburg and Berlin. She has been active in numerous capacities in film as well as in the arts, including with Thomas Draschan and TOMAK.

Camera

Martin Gschlacht, the Austrian director of photography, lives in Vienna. Graduate of the Vienna Film Academy. He has shot some thirty Austrian and international features with directors such as Jessica Hausner, Michael Glawogger or Shirin Neshat among others. He has earned numerous prizes and is founding member of coop99 filmproduktion. "In the Basement" is the first film he worked on with Ulrich Seidl.

Hans Selikovsky studied cinematography at the Film School in Vienna. He is the acclaimed director of photography of numerous films including "Müllers Büro" (Müller's Office), "Indien" (India) and "Requiem für Dominik" (Requiem for Dominic). He first collaborated with Ulrich Seidl on the director's debut theatrical feature, "Good News", later working on such as "Der Busenfreund" (The Bosom Friend), "Models", "Tierische Liebe" (Animal Love) and "PARADIES: Glaube" (PARADISE: Faith).

Wolfgang Thaler, born in 1958. Award-winning Austrian cameraman and professor at the Film Academy. He has collaborated with Ulrich Seidl since 1998, standing behind the camera on, among others, "Hundstage" (Dog Days), "Jesus, du weißt" (Jesus, You Know), "Import Export" and the "PARADISE" trilogy.

“In the Basement”

The photographs in this book are images taken from footage shot for Ulrich Seidl’s “In the Basement” (Im Keller).

Austria 2014, 85 min
Director: Ulrich Seidl
Idea and concept: Ulrich Seidl, Veronika Franz
Camera: Martin Gschlacht
Additional camera: Hans Selikovsky
Second additional camera: Wolfang Thaler
Sound: Ekkehart Baumung
Editor: Christoph Brunner
Artistic collaborator: Veronika Franz
Production manager: Louis Oellerer, Max Linder
Line producer: Konstantin Seitz
Producer: Ulrich Seidl
Cast: Fritz Lang, Alfreda Klebinger, Manfred Ellinger, Inge Ellinger, Josef Ochs, Alessa Duchek, Gerald Duchek, Cora Kitty, Peter Vokurek, Walter Holzer et al.

Production: Ulrich Seidl Film Produktion and coop99 filmproduktion
With support from: Österreichisches Filminstitut, Filmfonds Wien, ORF (Film/Fernseh-Abkommen), Land Niederösterreich
Co-produced by: WDR
In collaboration with: ARTE

Synopsis

The film is about people and their obsessions.
The film is about basements and what people do in them in their free time.
The film is about brass-band music and opera arias, expensive furniture and cheap men's jokes, sexuality and sadism, fitness and fascism, whips and dolls, snakes and guns, love and the longing for love.

Acknowledgement

For their contribution to the publication of this book, Ulrich Seidl and the editors Claus Philipp and Astrid Wolfig sincerely thank Roland Teichmann, Director of the Austrian Film Institute, Gerlinde Seitner, Managing Director of the Vienna Film Fund, and Erwin Pröll, Governor of Lower Austria.

Colophon

Editors
Claus Philipp, Astrid Wolfig

Editorial Department
Veronika Franz

Production Manager Ulrich Seidl Film Produktion
Louis Oellerer

Frames
Ulrich Seidl, Martin Gschlacht, Hans Selikovsky, Wolfgang Thaler

Authors
Olaf Möller, Franz Schuh, Ute Woltron, Herbert Lachmayer,
Claus Philipp, Markus Keuschnigg

Translation German - English
Robert Gray, Montréal

Translation Editor
Joan Irving

Translation Revisors
Christa Japel and Hildegard Grüter

Graphic Design
Bruno Margreth, Laura Vuille, Zürich

Lithography
Heer Druck AG, Sulgen

Printing
Heer Druck AG, Sulgen

Bookbinder
Buchbinderei Burkhardt AG, Mönchaltorf

With Support from:
Österreichisches Filminstitut
Filmfonds Wien
Land Niederösterreich
Ulrich Seidl Film Produktion

ISBN 978-3-7165-1815-1
BENTELI Verlag, Sulgen
www.benteli.ch

German Edition
Ulrich Seidl. Im Keller
ISBN 978-3-7165-1799-4